FCO²®

The *Ultimate* formula
for a happy life

FCO²®

The *Ultimate* formula for a happy life

The Handbook to Personal Happiness

Bruce Lawson

BAHons, MPRACNLP, PRAC EFT, GQHP

Matador
9 De Montfort Mews
Leicester LE1 7FW, UK
Tel: (+44) 116 255 9311 / 9312
Email: books@troubador.co.uk
Web: www.troubador.co.uk/matador

ISBN 978-1904744-016

Typeset in 11pt Gill by Troubador Publishing Ltd, Leicester, UK
Printed in the UK by The Cromwell Press Ltd, Trowbridge, Wilts, UK

Matador is an imprint of Troubador Publishing Ltd

*This book is dedicated to my two daughters,
Dafna and Galia, who are a constant source
of inspiration and pride*

Contents

Preface

Welcome to FCO^2 the ultimate formula for a happy life and your journey to a better existence.

My name is Bruce Lawson and I will be your guide on this quest.

As we begin our journey together you may be wondering how this simple formula FCO^2 can really be described as the ultimate formula for a happy life.

As I hope you will see, as together we explore this formula in this our voyage of discovery, that the three components used singly and together harmonise to ensure that in everything you need to do in life you CAN ensure success and happiness.

These three components are: FOCUS, CONGRUENCE and CONTROL: and if all three are practiced effectively and together, you will find that the gift of a happy life will be there for you now and for always; whatever the situation you find yourself.

So relax, sit back, get comfortable as we go through the Ultimate formula for a happy life; and I hope you enjoy the journey as much as I did when I created the formula and identified the signposts to happiness.

Bruce Lawson
January 2007
Kent.

Acknowledgements

This book developed out of a journey of exploration which began with my experiences during my NLP and contemporary psychotherapy training. This set me on the road which led to reading much of a spiritual nature from Tibetan and native American texts through to contemporary psychology. The signposts along the way which led to where I now stand were many but those that really lit up my way are Steven Gilligan, whose books and workshop were so powerful an experience and a variety of Buddhist and monastic teachings. The synergy of all this came together in this book. May it fill your life with sunrises.

CHAPTER I

Introduction
How the components fit together

We begin by looking at each of the three components in brief and understand what each one's function is and how they fit together to form the ultimate formula for a happy life. Then we will look at each component individually in depth. Finally we will bring all the elements together as our journey reaches its first major milestone on the road to a happier life.

Focus

So-the first element in our formula is "F" which stands for…. Focus. Without understanding and applying this fundamental principle it is impossible to live a happy life.

Focus is about concentration on an identified and clear goal. Focus is the Laser beam that cuts through life's detritus. Focus is the shining light that illuminates the path we want to take. Finally, Focus directs our steps on the right path and stops us straying onto what might appear a more attractive or easier way. Focus allows us to hear the real tune clearly and helps us block out all that background noise or siren song; tempting us away from the purity of the correct beat.

Of course there are certain essential elements for us to be able to focus which we will explore later:

First is identifying a clear goal.

Second is clarifying a clear path to achieve that goal.

Third is deciding what resources are needed to begin that journey.

Fourth is taking the first steps.

Fifth is sticking to the journey till the destination is reached, whatever the roadblocks put in your way, by Focusing on the **NOW**.

Congruent

The second component In our formula is being **CONGRUENT**.

Even though Focus is vital to achieving a happy life, without the element of being Congruent, your Focus will slip away and you will find it ever more difficult to stay on the right path.

Being Congruent means that all elements of your being are working harmoniously, together for the common goal.

When you are Congruent you will find you are happier, have more energy and life will feel like a continuous beautiful sunrise.

As I said, being Congruent is about all of your being working in harmony towards a common goal-That is Mind, Body and Soul, or whatever labels you may have for these three elements of your being.

Control

CONTROL is the third component. You will only be able to stay focused and congruent if you are also able to exercise Control. But what do we mean by "Control"? When we look at some of the most common pressures in our life that can cause Stress, Anxiety or Depression; a common factor in our negative reaction is a Loss of Control. WE FEEL events, or other people are controlling us and so we feel helpless, powerless, diminished. So, asserting and maintaining Control is a vital element in a happy life and combined with Focus and Congruence our other two components it completes our *Ultimate Formula for a Happy Life.*

As we will see later, Control is both Physical and Psychological and it provides the framework or skeleton for our other two components Focus and Congruence.

Control is our script in life's play, our map on our journey, our score to our musical. When we develop and maintain Control, we take responsibility for ourselves and our lives and it allows us to stay Focused, be Congruent and move forward in an Honest, Open, Positive and Happy way.

ISN'T THAT WHAT WE ALL REALLY WANT??

So there we have it, FCO^2 – The Ultimate formula for a happy life is about Focus, Congruence and Control. When all three elements are combined together, whatever our situation, however difficult the problems we face; applying this formula will allow you to lead a positive, happy, honest life, fulfilling your true potential, making the most of very opportunity, every step on your journey, living fully in the

NOW as opposed to dwelling on the past or wasting time dreaming of the future.

I would like to end this introduction with a true story:

For years I had been involved quite happily in training and coaching yet though I earned a good living and enjoyed my work, I always knew that there was something more: It felt like a dull ache in my stomach, a ghost I knew was there but just out of view; like a tune not quite remembered. Then one day, in a study group, we did an exercise to define where we really wanted to be in life.

As I completed the exercise it was as if a weight had lifted; all of a sudden a light shone, my body and my mind felt completely in synch and I knew without a shadow of a doubt that guidance and counselling, helping people to be happy was my real life focus and goal.

That realisation energised me physically and emotionally. When you are on the right path everything is Congruent and you walk out from the shadows of your insecurity or unsureness into the wonderful light of honest, positive knowledge and action. Its like the first time you fall in love; all your Focus, feelings and emotions are heightened and the world becomes a better place.

This is what you too can achieve when you follow this path, apply this formula FCO^2 – which really is the Ultimate formula for a happy life as I am sure you will see… SO, ARE YOU READY TO BEGIN OUR JOURNEY.. and absorb the detail that will help YOU achieve all that you truly want for yourself? I do hope so.

So, to get you ready I want you to be totally relaxed and focused so you get the most out of this handbook. Please read the script in the appendix to help you gain relaxed focus.

CHAPTER 2

Focus

Now we begin our detailed journey to a happier life. The first element we will explore together is Focus. What it is, how to get it, how to maintain it and how to use it.

The five elements

As I said, Focus is the searchlight that illuminates the path, banishes the shadows and lights up the dark; however to turn the light on, to tune it, **we first need to identify a clear goal.** This is the first of five elements that make up our focus element. To remind you the other four are:

2. Clarifying a clear path to achieve the goal

3. Deciding on the resources needed to achieve that goal, then

4. Taking the first step and finally

5. Sticking to the journey, ignoring the roadblocks, Focusing on the NOW till our destination is reached.

So, how do we achieve our first element of Focus –

identifying a clear goal? Simple to say, this is one of the hardest and most fundamental elements in the whole formula and it is essential to get it right.

The most important thing is, you will have to be completely honest with yourself when you identify your clear goal. It **must be a goal you truly want to achieve for yourself**; not a goal others want you to go for or are pushing you to attain.

For example: I knew a parent who always wanted to be a professional footballer and never quite made it. He pushed his son all through his early years and teens to practice, play and try out for the local team. The problem was his son hated football and wanted to be a musician. For twelve years he forced himself to obey his father till finally a team rejected him; he had a case of depression and it was only during this phase of his life that through a series of events he was finally able to talk to his father about what **he** wanted. His father had never realised his son's true desire. It was only after they had these discussions that the father realised his son's real goals and that the son was able to pursue his true goal. His depression lifted and now he is a successful musician. There are many such examples.

You must identify **your** clear goal that is right for **you**.

So, be honest that the goal is your goal.

If you are still having trouble identifying that goal, try this: imagine where you would like to be in one, five and ten year's time. Really imagine where you are at that time, what job you are doing, your personal situation, your geographical location. How much do you want or need to earn for the life you really want in the future?

Spend time, imagine a number of situations in as much detail as you can. If it helps, write them down or record them. As you complete this exercise, and there is no time limit to it, one of the scenarios will feel right; like trying on a piece of clothing that fits like a glove; or hearing a piece of music that resonates in your soul and makes the hairs stand up on your neck. A picture that speaks to your very being. That is the scenario; that is the one-that is your honest goal now identified. Don't second guess it or criticise it intellectually. Think it again, feel it – does it feel right? If it does, without emotional reservation, then it is the right goal for you to pursue.

So, whether it takes five minutes or five months you now have your identified goal-Well done Congratulations. Remember, the second element of Focus is **Clarifying A Clear Path To Achieve That Goal.** Once your goal is clear it is now necessary to illuminate the path that will lead you to that goal. Now is the time to organise your thoughts and life with the **end** in mind.

Your goal is the light you must constantly head towards, the tune in your head that always stays with you. Your life is now bounded by your goal and how to reach it. Everything that contributes to the path that will let you reach your goal must be embraced; anything that distracts or slows you on your journey or tries to divert you must be ruthlessly put aside.

In this, your inner journey and your outer voyage; for you and you alone; there can be no excuses. Deviation is **not** an option; prevarication or delay is to be rejected.

With this in mind the clarity of the path will depend on how rigorously you decide where the path needs to lead to achieve your goal. What elements do you need to consider in order to gain that clarity?

Well, Timescale – how long honestly do you need to achieve your goal? What do you need to change or improve or even reject in your life for the path to be clear, uncluttered and free of obstruction and diversion?

This could mean a change of job, personal circumstances, even, as the path becomes clearer, a geographical move. To a new home, county even country.

These are all tough decisions but being honest and focused on your goal means you must sweep the path clean and stick to it, whatever it takes: otherwise you will be unable to apply the ultimate formula for a happy life.

Let me end this section by telling you a story which illustrates how important a clear path is to find and stick to. Before that however I want to teach you an exercise which might help you in reinforcing the goal you have chosen, clarifying the path and keeping you motivated on the journey whatever the difficulties. Read it through, then, if it helps, record it onto your MP3 so you can listen to it later or any time you fancy. All the exercises are designed to be read out loud and recorded so you can play them back and listen to them.

Exercise

As always it begins with breathing. Sit in your chair:

Breathe in-hold for 2 seconds think count of 1 – breathe out slowly and deeply

Breathe in-hold for 2 seconds think count of 2 – breathe out slowly and deeply

Breathe in-hold for 2 seconds think count of 3 – breathe out slowly and deeply – and as you breathe out think about how your body is relaxing

Breathe in – hold for 2 seconds think count of 4 – breathe out slowly and deeply – and feel how heavy your feet feel against the ground

Breathe in-hold for 2 seconds think count of 5 – breathe out slowly and deeply – and feel how heavy your thighs feel against the chair and how relaxed

Breathe in – hold for 2 seconds think count of 6 – breathe out slowly and deeply – if your eyes feel heavy and you want to close them at any time DO SO NOW or whenever

Breathe in – hold for 2 seconds think count of 7 – breathe out slowly and deeply – and

feel how heavy and relaxed you back and bottom feel against the chair heavy and relaxed like your closed eyes

Breathe in – hold for 2 seconds think count of 8 – breathe out slowly and deeply – and feel how heavy your arms and shoulders feel heavy and totally relaxed with each breath

Breathe in – hold for 2 seconds think count of 9 – breathe out slowly and deeply – and feel how your whole body feel relaxed from your feet to your head relaxed yet focused

Breathe in – hold for 2 seconds think count of 10 – breathe out slowly and deeply – and feel how your mind is clear and ready to learn while your body stays totally relaxed

Now just keep breathing slowly and deeply while your mind stays deeply focused and your body continues to remain delightfully wonderfully relaxed.

Wonderful, now you are in the right frame to focus on the exercise of imagining you have achieved your goal. You can repeat this exercise whenever you want to reinforce your motivation to your goal.

I want you to imagine your goal and how

you will be when you have achieved it-whatever you have decided it is. SEE IT, EXPLORE ITS COLOURS, FEEL ITS EMOTIONS, ITS PHYSICALITY; LISTEN TO THE SOUNDS THAT SURROUND IT. And as your goal becomes more vibrant and clear, enjoy the wonderful depth of positive happiness, The deep emotion of well being achieving this goal gives. Take some time to explore your goal and the pleasure achieving it brings, the completeness, the peace, the satisfaction the inner calm. It is a warm woolly sweater that embraces and protects you, a harmonious sound that surrounds and relaxes you, a feeling of completeness and peace and warmth that keeps you safe and secure. Enjoy this, knowing you can return to it at any time.

AND NOW BEGIN TO WORK BACK MOVING IN TIME AND IMAGINE WHAT STEPS YOU NEED TO REACH THAT WONDERFUL GOAL. As you take each step back, look at each action necessary to keep you on that clear path to that goal. At each step, feel the emotional satisfaction of the right step and the right action on that path, the right decision made and stuck to. See each right decision, each correct step, its vibrant colour, listen to the positive sound of the right action stated aloud, and feel throughout your body how good and right each correct decision was following the right path reinforcing the road to your goal.

Carry on journeying back seeing each step, feeling each decision, sounding out every thought until you arrive at **TODAY**.

Now take a deep breath and in an instant review your journey. If that instant review makes you smile, makes your body feel good then you have your clear path. If anything strikes a sour note then stop. And when ready repeat the exercise till everything is congruent and you **KNOW** in every fibre of your body, mind and soul that your path is right, your aim is true.

Now you can open your eyes – enjoy the wonderful sensation of right focused decision and we can continue.

Please feel free to repeat this exercise any time you need to top up your motivation or give yourself a dose of warm wonder.

Now, as to the story I mentioned. A friend of mine decided their goal was to change career to develop skills that they had not used for a long time; to achieve that goal they realised they would need to change job. But when it came to it, fear of rejection, of not being offered another job or dropping their salary trapped them into staying where they were: years after they would be heard to say "If Only".

Don't you let yourself **Ever** say that. Life only exists in the NOW. Once focused on your true goal, clarify your path and stick to it. Otherwise instead of leading a happy fulfilled life, your life will be full of regret and lost opportunity.

As the poet said:

> "When the sun rises over the mountain top
> And the path to the summit is clear
> Only a fool waits for darkness to come
> As an excuse for his journey to fear
>
> The lit path in daylight
> Is clear and easily trod
> Hesitate not or the shadows
> Will obscure your surefooted way
> And tangents of dark and danger
> Will your journeys end defray" Bruce

So, there we are, we have identified a clear goal, and clarified our path to achieving that goal. Now we must embrace the third of the five elements of Focus and that is:

Deciding on the resources needed to achieve our goal

Before we look at this element, how is your breathing? Are you still feeling relaxed and focused?

What do you need to achieve your goal? It might be that one of those resources is to be fit. If this is a resource you need, then do you need to join a gym or can you achieve that resource by walking or other exercise? A resource for that of course will be to schedule your time so you have enough to achieve your fitness level. Resource on resource, fitness needs time and time in itself is a valuable resource that shouldn't be wasted on your journey.

Other resources you might need could be; money, a vehicle, maybe a business partner or some skill you need to acquire to reach that goal of yours. Whatever the resources you need- how many and varied they may be to help you reach your goal and to clarify and stay on your path; you must list the resources you really need and ensure they are all in place at whatever part of the journey they are needed.

Think of a film director; they need to plan out all the equipment, cameras and so on, location, scripts costumes and props before they can start filming otherwise they will be unable to complete their project or shoot their film. You are your own director: make sure you list, manage and use your resources wisely. If you do, you will be able to stick to your clear path and achieve your goal.

So, there we have it; the first three elements of Focus are completed. The fourth is both simple and sometimes the most difficult. That is:

Taking the first step on your path to your goal. It is said that the longest journey begins with a single step and that is just as true in your epic journey to reach your goal. Many people allow their own fears and insecurities to hold them back and block their chance to achieve happiness. It is absolutely essential that once you have identified your goal, defined your clear path and gathered your resources that you do indeed take that first vital step.

Too many people plan but are unable to put that plan into action. Your focus, your honesty and belief will let you take that first step. As long as your goal is clear and honest then you owe it to yourself to walk towards it.

No symphony exists till the first note is played; no journey begins till the first step; no painting till brush touches canvas. So do not hesitate – Apply the old Latin phrase "CARPE DIEM" – Seize the day – Live in the Now – Don't Hope – ACT.

Take that first step, and once you have, you will be closer to your goal. Your focus will intensify with every step after that. Look forward, not back, do not tarry, don't let others divert you, stay with your focus to achieve your goal and the **happiness you deserve**!! And that is how taking the first step beautifully merges into the final aspect of Focus – that is the fifth element: **Sticking to your journey.**

So, to conclude our exploration of the first of our three elements to the formula – Focus, let us dwell a minute on the fifth part of Focus – **Sticking to your Journey**.

As we have said, you have begun your quest on your road to happiness, your goal is the motorway sign that directs you, the view of the mountain peak that inspires you and the epic piece of music that continues to sound in your head. Keep those signs, images, sounds and feelings always with you. They are your map – in all you do, in every action you take, every word you utter, every feeling you experience ask yourself one thing and one thing alone. Does this take me closer to my goal, help me achieve what I seek or will it divert me from my route or mean it takes longer to reach what I seek. If it takes you closer, embrace it without hesitation. If it seeks to divert you, distract you, or delay you; reject it immediately. If you concentrate on the positive, live life in the Now and act always in pursuit of your goal and reject diversion, then you will stick to your journey, stay on the right path and reach your goal faster, making your route to happiness stronger, more profound and more worthwhile.

So my friends, there we have it, we have completed our exploration of the first of our three Prime elements in the ultimate formula for a happy life. You now understand, I hope, the importance of Focus and how applying it as we have explored it will help you reach the happiness you seek.

Before we begin on the second Prime element of our formula: **Being Congruent**.

Do not attempt to absorb all of this at once. Rest. until you are ready to continue or: take a minute to enjoy a moment of rest and relaxation. To help you why not use the relaxation script at the end of this book, record it onto your MP3.

CHAPTER 3
Being Congruent

So the next prime element of FCO^2 is Being **CONGRUENT.**

Fully relaxed and focused, now join me in our next part of our journey, the second element of our ultimate formula for a happy life – Being Congruent.

Let me start with a story: well two stories really. The first one concerns a friend of mine. We will call him James.

James had a successful career in the city. For ten

years he had concentrated on his career, been successful and climbed the corporate ladder. In his late 30s he had a great salary, lovely house and a lovely partner. Yet more and more, as he travelled to work each day it seemed to, get harder, to take more energy. Rather than waking up in the morning energised and looking forward to his day, he felt like a stone was dragging him down and draining his energy and enthusiasm away.

He tried to ignore it, do his job, enjoy his lifestyle but he realised something wasn't right. Finally he decided to talk to his partner about it. His partner asked when he had begun to feel this way. During that conversation he realised it had started when he had come back from a business meeting. He had been walking back to the train station through a new part of town he didn't know. Then he remembered, he had seen a guy sitting on the pavement, obviously sleeping rough. As he walked past, he had noticed that although his clothes were old and dirty his shoes were shining. As he stopped to look, the guy looked up at him, saw where he was staring and said, "I was a soldier once, old habits die hard." And then as James went to walk away the ex soldier said "Remember... we were real people once." James had suppressed that memory but now, in conversation with his partner he realised it had been eating away at him, at his soul since that moment.

As the memory and feelings came to the fore, James realised what he really wanted, **NO** needed to do, was change his job and focus on helping people like that old soldier. With his partner's support he left his high paid city job, joined a charity as an organiser and since then every day when he gets up, his energy and enthusiasm are high. Why, because he knows in his mind, body and soul that he is doing what he really wants to do. He is not satisfying his material needs while ignoring his spiritual and emotional side. He is finally **Congruent** and all his energies are aligned. So James feels complete, energised and happy: **THAT IS BEING CONGRUENT.**

Now ask yourself: is your job one that gets you up in the morning full of energy and hope? As you go to work are you looking forward to the day? And at work are you filled with sunshine and positive energy? If you have answered YES, then it is quite likely that you are indeed Congruent, where your work is concerned. However, if you answered no, or not quite, then maybe you need to look at what you do? Is it materially satisfying but emotionally destructive? Are you trapped in a routine, scared to break out? Does your work drain rather than energise? If this is the case, then like so many you are not Congruent and you are suffering from an energy drain because your mind, body and soul are not in alignment. You may get more sick more often, take more absence, suffer from headaches, have trouble sleeping, feel depressed or apathetic. If this is you, then you are not congruent and for your total health and happiness you need to change your focus, become congruent and take control.

By the end of this handbook you WILL have the tools to be happy; so take a deep breath, adjust your breathing, relax and read my second story.

This story concerns someone we will call Jane. Jane had met her partner when she was quite young. He had been her first real boyfriend and she had now been with him seven years. Being always conscious of her weight, Jane felt grateful to her partner for being with her even though he regularly highlighted her weight and the fact that she was lucky he was with her, as no one else would find her attractive.

Over the years Jane had become dependent on her boyfriend and the more time passed the more controlling he became, until Jane only went out with HIM, had few friends, and didn't socialise at work because she felt she had to get back home to be there for her partner and cook his meal. Jane had tried to diet many times but it never seemed to work; and each time it failed, her partner would make sure to point out her failure and how lucky she was that he was around.

Though Jane felt she loved her partner, after seven years Jane felt empty, depressed, had a low self esteem and image and felt life was just drifting by.

One day, at lunch, with one of her few work friends, the friend showed her an article. The article was about how certain women were strong and independent. The most amazing thing to Jane was that two of the women featured with their pictures showed them to be considerably larger than her.

Jane began to question, how could this be, that these larger women were also independent and strong? She thought about it all night and the next day, at lunch with the same friend, started to talk about it. Her friend was thrilled with Jane discussing this subject and told her she had always wanted to tell her that she thought she looked lovely and did not have nearly as much of a problem as Jane thought she had.

Like a ripple caused by a stone thrown into a pool, Jane began to question her own assumptions of lack of self worth, weight and dependence. Over the coming months she started a diet programme, joined a gym and improved her clothes sense. Not surprisingly, her partner was unsupportive and negative as he felt his control slipping away. Finally Jane had the courage to end the relationship.

As she told her friend: "The day I left him and moved

into my own place, I felt a weight had been lifted; going to the gym, I have met some wonderful friends. I am more fit than ever, have lost some weight, though that's not so important. What is fantastic is how much energy I seem to have. Not just physical but emotional, the world seems a better place, even my job is more fun."

Jane had discovered the joy of being Congruent, of going from a dependent, safe but debilitating relationship and low self image; which drained and depressed her; to a congruent life where mind, body and soul were in harmony, and where she discovered the true energy of happiness and being congruent.

So, my friends, ask yourself, and be honest; do your relationships make you feel loved, wanted, energised? Do they support and nurture you? If they do then it sounds to me like you are definitely enjoying congruent personal lives. Congratulations.

However, if any of your relationships are draining you. If you feel used or manipulated instead of energised and supported, if guilt and blame are the basis, rather than love and support, then I would say you are definitely NOT Congruent. However safe or superficially secure or loving these relationships appear; for your own health and happiness, you need to examine if you are in the right place, and whether you need to change the relationship or its structure. If you don't, it will be very difficult to experience the happiness, energy and health you deserve.

Only you know the truth – and this handbook will help you identify and follow the path you really want to be on; the goal you truly seek; and the congruent life you deserve.

So, there we have it, two stories about being congruent. I hope you begin to understand the positive power when you are congruent and the negative energy sapping state when you are not. With that in mind, let us explore different types of being congruent in more detail. By the way – how is your breathing? Are you still relaxed and focused?

So what is being Congruent? Well, to be congruent we need to be in harmony of mind, body and soul; or if you prefer, physical, emotional and psychological harmony. Let's look at being congruent in each of these three elements and then combine those to examine what is being totally congruent.

While we look at these elements of being congruent, I want you to consider something. **Being congruent takes no willpower.** You have heard people say – Oh yes I stuck to the diet through sheer willpower; or, I finished that race on pure willpower, or even, you need willpower to stop drinking or smoking.

If you need willpower to achieve anything, then you are not congruent, and you are fighting against yourself. You can never win that battle in the long run, which is why so many short term gains end up as long term disasters. Think about that as we explore being congruent in more detail.

Physical Congruence

With that mind, let us first look at physical congruence or being congruent in our body. I wonder what you are imagining now when I tell you that being congruent in your body, physical congruence is essential for true health and happiness. Being congruent is about harmony; it is a reflection of an uninterrupted flow of energy. Like a river flowing swiftly along its course, or a piece of music played flawlessly without interruption; the energy is free, natural and unforced.

So how does this relate to your body, to the physical? Have you guessed yet? Well there are several elements to your body being congruent. There is Food or Diet; that is diet with a small "D". Don't worry, this is not another diet fad. There is exercise; then there is sleep, freedom from stress and relaxation. For perfect physical congruence all these need to be balanced correctly. Get these elements right and your energy will flow free and you will be on the way to health and happiness. Get them wrong and you set up for yourself numerous blocks and dams that will interrupt your energy flow and health.

So did I mention anything you were already thinking about, maybe added one or two elements? Well let's see how they fit together to help you gain physical congruence, being congruent in your body.

Food

The first element is Food. I am not going to lecture you as to diet; there is enough information available now from many sources to help you decide what you should eat. So let's be honest with each other, forget fad diets. Do you know why they only work, if at all, generally in the short term? Because you need willpower to stay on them. And as we have said-if you need willpower, you are fighting against yourself, so you can never win. That's why whatever your weight, if you have tried diets, you have probably tried many. They work for a short time and then your old eating habit re-asserts itself. That is because you are not congruent and the incorrect eating pattern is not a problem to be cured, merely a symptom of other areas where you are struggling. Cure those and you will become congruent and eating correctly will no longer be a problem.

You only need to stick to a couple of basic rules

where food is concerned to help you be physically congruent:

1. To lose weight or not increase it, energy intake must be less than energy used or expended. In other words, don't eat more calories than you can burn off in day. Adjust how much you eat or how much you exercise so that the equation is either equal, to maintain your weight, or less on your intake, to reduce it. In the end it really is that basic, anyone **can** do it, so why don't we? Its not the diet, it's the other areas where we are not congruent we need to fix. However, in the meantime, till these are fixed, start to apply the formula I mentioned, to help you on your journey to physical congruence.

2. We are what we eat. If you want your body to have energy and keep healthy then its obvious you need to eat the right food. If a car has to run it needs the right fuel, otherwise it performs badly or breaks down. Our bodies are no different. So it really is not rocket science to know that eating fresh fruit, vegetables, lean meats like chicken and fish and keeping alcohol and drugs like coffee and tea to sensible levels is only common sense. If you exist on a diet of fast food, pre prepared meals and junk food then your body will be unable to give you the energy and health you need. You certainly cannot be congruent and you will not be healthy and happy.

That's all there is to the secret of the link between food and being congruent except one last thing. If you are saying to yourself "I don't have time or the money to eat healthily", take a moment to check out how long it takes to boil vegetables, grill a piece of chicken or fish or boil or bake a potato. You will find it's cheaper to eat sensibly, takes no more time and you will be doing yourself a power of good. Try it for a week; if after that you feel less energy and less positive than before then go back to your old ways. I know you **will** feel better, more positive, more energised. Do what you feel is honestly right for you and you will gain the benefits.

So, how are we doing? Hopefully your mind is focused, absorbing these ideas while your breathing and your body remain relaxed. If you need to take a five minute break, make yourself a cup of something, have a stretch, please do so and I will see you in a minute.

Exercise

Welcome back. The second element in being physically congruent is to do with exercise. We have already seen that exercise and food are related. To be physically congruent your body needs to be maintained. It's like our friend the car. If you don't turn over the engine regularly or charge the battery then when you do need to use it, it will let you down. It's the same with our bodies. They need exercise, so that all the muscles, including the heart are kept in good condition.

Again, I am not saying you need to spend a fortune joining a gym and working out five times a week – unless of course you want to. However, you should grab every opportunity to exercise. Even if it's walking up stairs instead of using a lift; maybe you are stuck at a desk at your work most of the day. Use any breaks you have to walk, outside, round the office whatever, don't just sit there, get your muscles working. Try walking at weekends or maybe cycling if you enjoy that. If you have the chance to swim or go to the gym as well that is an added bonus. Whatever you do, whatever your budget or lifestyle, make exercise a natural and welcome part of your day. Establish a routine, even if its only ten minutes a day so the exercise allows you to keep your body in trim. Do this, and combined with the other elements we have mentioned you will achieve physical congruence.

So there we are; we have covered Food and Exercise. It really is quite simple; yet like so many things in life it is not the complexity that stops us, just the awareness and FOCUS to take action. Exercise like diet should not take willpower, because it should be a natural and desired part of your life.

Sleep

The Third element in being physically congruent is Sleep. Let me ask you: how well do you sleep at night? We all need different amounts – are you getting enough sleep? If you are and you wake refreshed and energised then please feel free to skip this bit. However, if your sleep is fitful or interrupted; if you have trouble switching off and getting to sleep without resort to pills or alcohol then stay with me. Lack of sleep is another symptom of your body telling you, you are **not congruent**.

It is a result of other elements where you are not congruent interfering with your energy patterns. Till we fix those elements lets at least help you to get a decent night's sleep. You cannot be physically and therefore completely congruent if you are not getting enough sleep. As you know, lack of sleep leads to irritation, mistakes, tiredness, depression and a massive energy drain. It is a major block to being congruent, to letting our energy flow naturally; so let's see if we can help you get your good night's visit to slumberland.

One of the most common causes of being unable to drop off to sleep is one of the mind racing. If you can't switch off, you can't fall asleep. So let's try an exercise to help those of you that have that problem. What I suggest is that you try the exercise now, and then tonight, before you try to go to sleep do it again to help yourself drop off. Read it as many times as you need until you feel able to do it on your own. By that time you should be entering the land of nod quite easily.

Before we do the exercise, some obvious points. Don't drink coffee or other stimulants less than four hours before you go to bed. Don't eat a full meal two to three hours before going to sleep; your body needs to be drug free and not having to digest a heavy meal, otherwise all the energy and relaxation to help you sleep will be channelled elsewhere. Ok – so for this exercise you need to be lying on your bed, ready for sleep. Lie on your back, lights dim or off and with no distractions if possible like the radio or TV; noisy neighbours, screaming kids – you get the idea. Are you ready, lying on your back, comfortable, excellent then lets begin. Again feel free to record this onto your MP3.

Exercise

This is an exercise in relaxation of body and mind and by the end you will be able to fall naturally into a deep relaxed sleep. As you are lying there first begin by getting your breathing slow and steady. You know how. Breathe in slowly and deeply hold for two seconds and breathe out fully. Lets first repeat that ten times to get you full relaxed
Then after that we will use tensing and relaxing our body to ensure you fall easily and naturally into a wonderful deep satisfying sleep. At any time when you feel yourself slipping into sleep let it happen, you do not need to complete the exercise just let the recorded mp3 run on in the background as you fall deeply asleep.

SO – Breathe in – hold for 2 seconds think count of 1 – breathe out slowly and deeply

Breathe in – hold for 2 seconds think count of 2 – breathe out slowly and deeply

Breathe in – hold for 2 seconds think count of 3 – breathe out slowly and deeply – and as you breathe out think about how your body is relaxing

Breathe in – hold for 2 seconds think count of 4 – breathe out slowly and deeply – and feel how heavy your feet feel resting on the bed

Breathe in – hold for 2 seconds think count of 5 – breathe out slowly and deeply – and feel how heavy your thighs feel against the bed and how relaxed

Breathe in – hold for 2 seconds think count of 6 – breathe out slowly and deeply – if your eyes feel heavy and you want to close them at any time **DO SO NOW** or whenever

Breathe in – hold for 2 seconds think count of 7 – breathe out slowly and deeply – and feel how heavy and relaxed you, back and bottom feel against the bed, heavy and relaxed like your closed eyes

Breathe in – hold for 2 seconds think count of 8 – breathe out slowly and deeply – and feel how heavy your arms and shoulders feel, heavy and totally relaxed with each breath

Breathe in – hold for 2 seconds think count of 9 – breathe out slowly and deeply – and feel how your whole body feel, relaxed from your feet to your head, relaxed at peace

Breathe in – hold for 2 seconds think count of 10 – breathe out slowly and deeply – and feel how your mind is quiet and ready for sleep while your body stays deeply totally relaxed

Now just keep breathing slowly and deeply while your mind stays deeply quiet and your body continues to remain delightfully wonderfully deeply relaxed.

Wonderful, keeping your breathing relaxed and slow feel yourself drifting off into sleep.

Start with your toes and tense and relax your left toes twice, that's it, tense and relax, tense and relax.

Now your left foot, tense and relax, tense and relax.

Now move up to your left leg, tense and relax, tense and relax,

Now your left thigh, tense and relax, tense and relax; that's it, feel how wonderfully heavy and relaxed your body is and how peaceful and quiet your mind is, still focusing just on my voice on tensing and relaxing nothing else..

Now your chest, tense and relax tense and relax, that's it..

Now your left shoulder, tense and relax, tense and relax,

Now your left arm, tense and relax, tense

and relax, yes and now your left hand, tense and relax, tense and relax, excellent slowly drifting to sleep your body wonderfully heavy, your eyes heavy and relaxed, your mind at peace as you clench and relax your eyelids tense and relax as your eyes stay firmly deeply shut...

And now the right side of your body as before starting with your right toes:

Start with your toes and tense and relax your right toes twice, that's it tense and relax, tense and relax.

Now your right foot, tense and relax, tense and relax.

Now move up to your right leg, tense and relax, tense and relax,

Now your right thigh, tense and relax, tense and relax; that's it feel how wonderfully heavy and relaxed your body is and how peaceful and quiet your mind is still focusing just on my voice on tensing and relaxing nothing else..

Now your chest tense and relax tense and relax, that's it..

Now your right shoulder tense and relax, tense and relax.

Now your right arm, tense and relax, tense and relax yes and

Now your right hand, tense and relax, tense and relax, excellent, slowly drifting to sleep, your body wonderfully heavy, your eyes heavy and relaxed, your mind at peace as you clench and relax your eyelids tense and relax as your eyes stay firmly deeply shut... as you fall into a deep relaxed warm and wonderful natural sleep, sleeping through the night your body and mind rested and at peace so that you will wake refreshed and energised ready for a wonderful new day.

Welcome back and I hope you found that exercise, pleasant and effective. So, to return to physical congruence. We have looked at three of the elements; diet, exercise and sleep; there are two more essential elements in keeping your body physically congruent.

Free from Stress and Relaxation

The fourth and fifth elements are linked and they are: **Being Free From Stress and Knowing How To Relax.** You may not know, but there is a physical cost to being stressed, especially if you are one of the many people who suffer from various forms of stress over a long period. We will look at the emotional and psychological cost later. For the moment consider this: Every time you allow yourself to get stressed there are chemical changes and physical changes in your body. All these changes help in accelerating the aging process. So you need to realise, if you are one of those people that do suffer from stress, that you are helping yourself age faster and subjecting your body to an unhealthy state.

The whole subject of stress is a book and CD in itself; suffice it to say here, that when you get stressed, chemicals such as Adrenaline and Cortisol flood your body. These chemicals are designed to prepare the body for what is known as the Fight or Flight response, that is they speed up the body's metabolism, the heart beats faster, blood pressure increases [which is why some of you suffer from headaches when you get stressed] and the body goes into overdrive. That is all very well in small bursts, but over time it wears the body down. These chemicals also, by the way, suppress the immune system, so stressed people leave themselves open to a greater risk of illness.

At the same time, if you think back to when you

have been stressed, or uptight; maybe in your car stuck in a traffic jam or on a crowded delayed train; you know what pushes your buttons. But here's the thing, remember how your body reacted. Were your hands clenched, shoulders taught, neck muscles tight, your stomach in knots? All of these are common physical manifestations of stress; and as I am sure you can realise, keeping those muscles under tension is bad for the body, burns energy unnecessarily and can lead to headaches and muscle pain.

So, bottom line, stress has a physical toll-to be physically congruent you NEED to reduce or eliminate becoming stressed, you NEED to be able to relax. So you can see how our fourth and fifth elements link. I believe, though we cannot control outside pressures of life; in most cases each of us has the capability to prevent that pressure turning into stress!

I am going to give you a few tips and an exercise to help you avoid stress, stay relaxed and allow yourself to stay physically congruent. The added plus is that you will reduce your ageing process, and allow your body's energy to flow productively. Stress is one of the blocks you need to eliminate to be physically congruent.

Triggers

There are two parts to preventing pressure leading to stress. The first is to identify what causes you stress; because once identified you can either avoid the cause or trigger; or learn how to reduce its effect. The second part is learning how to relax if you do feel stress creeping up on you.

So let's explore the first part. What are your triggers? They are those things in life that cause you to get stressed. They might be physical, at work or at home; emotional or behavioural. For example, I find that very overheated rooms start to get me very anxious. Once I realised that, I was able either to avoid such places or realise the source of the stress and leave the room before it became a problem. What about you? Is it confined spaces or crowds, noise or bright lights, computers that crash, your kids not tidying up their room or spending too long on the phone? What I suggest you do, now or when you are ready is; get a sheet of paper or a spreadsheet on your computer and write down all the physical, emotional or behavioural causes of your personal stress. Take your time, really think back to each cause-what actually triggered your stress? Write it down along with how it made you feel physically. Did you feel tense, muscles hunched, headache, whatever it may be. Once you have completed that exercise we will work on an exercise to help you deal with stress when you can't avoid the trigger.

Well, whether the list has one thing on it or one hundred, if you can't avoid or reduce the cause you need to know how to stop that pressure becoming stress and that is what these exercises are all about: Relaxing whatever the situation, whatever the problem. I am going to run through one exercise here which you can do walking, standing, sitting or lying. At the end of this handbook you will find a number of other exercises you can also use to help you relax.

As you have been reading this book you have already practiced relaxation techniques several times. This one is ideal to keep stress at bay and help you relax in any circumstance. Again feel free to record this onto your MP3.

Exercise

Whatever your physical posture we begin as always with the breathing:

Sit or stand or lie comfortably and relaxed, close your eyes if its safe to do so and allow yourself a few minutes of Total warm and complete relaxation free from any stress that might be near: let's just get our breathing relaxed too with this exercise you know so well now:

Breathe in – hold for 2 seconds think count of 1 – breathe out slowly and deeply

Breathe in – hold for 2 seconds think count of 2-breathe out slowly and deeply

Breathe in – hold for 2 seconds think count of 3 – breathe out slowly and deeply – and as you breathe out think about how your body is relaxing

Breathe in – hold for 2 seconds think count of 4 – breathe out slowly and deeply – and feel how heavy your feet feel against the ground – and now See your body as a strong oak tree. Your body is solid like the wide, brown trunk of the tree. Imagine sturdy roots growing from your legs and going down deeply into the earth, anchoring your body. You feel solid and strong, able to handle any stress.

Breathe in – hold for 2 seconds think count of 5 – breathe out slowly and deeply – and feel how heavy your thighs feel and how relaxed and strong anchored to the earth like a strong wide powerful oak tree you feel

Breathe in – hold for 2 seconds think count of 6 – breathe out slowly and deeply – if your eyes feel heavy and you want to close them at any time **DO SO NOW** or whenever letting your energy flow through you, grounding you to the earth as an oak tree as its roots stay grounded to the earth

Breathe in – hold for 2 seconds think count of 7 – breathe out slowly and deeply – and feel how heavy and relaxed the rest of your body feels with energy flowing from top to bottom, relaxed and calm grounded in the earth as the oak tree, strong and powerful.

Breathe in – hold for 2 seconds think count of 8 – breathe out slowly and deeply – and feel how heavy your arms and shoulders feel heavy and totally relaxed with each breath, energy flowing calmly through from your head to your toes, your feet in contact with the ground, grounded in the earth as the oak tree has its roots grounded in the soil.

Breathe in – hold for 2 seconds think count of 9 – breathe out slowly and deeply – and feel how your whole body feels relaxed from your feet to your head, relaxed yet focused

Breathe in – hold for 2 seconds think count of 10 – breathe out slowly and deeply – and feel how your mind is clear and calm free from tension or stress, your body and mind ready to continue whatever the situation, grounded an calm, strong as the oak, grounded and aware and safe and secure as the oak tree, able to stay calm and relaxed whatever the situation.

Now just keep breathing slowly and deeply while your mind stays deeply calm your body continues to remain delightfully wonderfully relaxed.

Wonderful, now you are in the right frame to continue. Now you can open your eyes – enjoy the wonderful sensation of strength, and calm, totally relaxed and able to deal with whatever situation presents itself.

This is just one exercise combining relaxation, breathing and grounding techniques to keep you calm and relaxed whatever the pressure. Use it as often as you like and also use the other techniques at the end of this handbook.

This exercise can be used in private or in public really any place at any time you wish to. Practice it as often as you need to and I assure you life's pressures will not get you stressed; and if your diet is right, you get enough exercise and sleep and you are free from stress and can relax you will gain physical congruence, your body will be fully congruent and your energy flow will be uninterrupted. You will feel energised, happier and more positive about yourself and life in general and that's JUST PHYSICAL CONGRUENCE!

So when you are ready, breathing correctly and relaxed, let's continue and look at the Mind being congruent, in other words, psychological congruence. We will combine that with congruence of the soul or being emotionally congruent, because as you will see, the two are closely linked.

Psychological congruence

When we are not congruent in our mind and soul what tends to happen is we fight against ourselves; and as we have seen before, that is a battle none of us can win. Think about when you were last out shopping. You saw something in a shop you really fancied, but you knew, in your mind, you didn't need it or could not really afford it. That battle between your logical mind and your illogical feelings or emotion happens when we are not congruent. By the way, who won?? The trouble is, whoever won, You lost. What do I mean? Well, if you resisted buying the item your logical mind felt good but your soul felt cheated. If you did buy the item then your soul and emotions felt temporarily fulfilled until your mind reminds you how weak you were not to resist. You see, when you fight yourself you never win! However, to continue the example, if you knew you needed an item for yourself, or as a gift for another, say you decided to donate to your favourite charity. You knew how much you could afford and you donated that amount. Now, because mind and soul are congruent, you feel good about what you did. Not just for a brief moment, but forever. There is no down side because you were congruent; psychologically and emotionally in harmony. Your energy all flowed in one direction as opposed to pushing against itself.

For your mind and soul to be congruent there must be harmony between what you think and what you feel. If you are honest with yourself, and as we have seen before, you do need to be honest with yourself, you know when your mind and soul are in conflict. So how do we gain congruence over mind and soul? How do we harmonise our psychological attitudes and emotional responses? It's all about practice and awareness.

To start the process-from now on, every time you go to do something and there is a conflict between what you intend and what you desire; or if you think a thought, and your "Conscience" or your soul tells you its not right-**STOP! Take a deep breath and just take a few seconds to consider what it is causing the conflict.**

An example: You are in the office or at work and you are talking with your colleagues. As is normal, everyone is gossiping about someone else. You know a secret about the person under discussion. Your mind wants you to tell the group the secret but the voice of your soul, your conscience, reminds you that it is not really right to spread the information you learnt in confidence. Before you say anything, STOP. Take a breath and consider what is right for you, what will stop the conflict and bring congruence. It only takes a second and you know what is right. What is right is what is congruent. Act on that and you will feel an internal rush of energy and satisfaction that far outweighs the temporary few seconds buzz of being popular in a conversation.

When you have done this once and taken this first step of stopping and considering before action, you will be on the path to being more in tune and more in touch with yourself, the real you. Every time you do this it will get easier and easier to connect with the real honest hidden you that is your core you, your energised honest happy congruent self. Each time you recognise the tug between the psychological you and the emotional you and stop and resolve the conflict and resume the congruence of mind and soul you will release real energy into your being. You will feel more satisfied and you will KNOW: Yes I am better than that [that being the conflict or quick fix].

If you practice this awareness, the STOP, Breath; and act honestly, according to the congruent you; your conscience where mind and soul are in harmony; you will release that positive energy; feel better and be a better person. That will inevitably lead to a happier and healthier you. Believe me; people will begin to notice the difference. They will respect you more, listen to you more often, and whether you know it or not, react to the increased energy flow that such congruence brings.

So there we have it, being congruent in body, mind and soul, letting the energy flow freely through your physical, emotional and psychological self. Coupled to your Focus, being congruent will bring you a freedom and boost of energy every day you practice it. The wonderful thing is the more you practice it, the better and easier it gets. You will be healthier, happier, able to deal with life in a more positive and energised way and all around you will notice the difference.

Before we look at the final element in our Ultimate formula for a Happy life – Control; a couple of points.

I hope you can see now that willpower can only work in the short term because willpower is your mind imposing action on your body and soul. It is not congruent, so its only ever a short term success. Be congruent in your goal or task and you will never need willpower to achieve it. Tasks that are congruent take less effort and are more satisfying. To end this section on Congruence I would like you to consider the following poem:

> *"When mind and body fight*
> *And the soul inhabits only night*
> *When conscience is dismissed and quiet*
> *The essential you descends to riot.*
>
> *Energy flows not like a river straight*
> *But flux and barriers block its state*
> *And all in turmoil affects the mind*
> *Where headache rules and body's fined.*
>
> *Much better to bring harmony home*
> *Where mind and soul are free to roam*
> *As one united in body whole*
> *And congruence rule sour actions all*
> *Where our honest self does now stand tall."*
> Bruce

I hope you see that applying focus and being congruent can greatly increase your chances of health and happiness. All we need to do now is add one more element and the formula is complete. That element is Control. So please, feel free to take a break and come back refreshed for the final part of our Ultimate formula for a happy life.

CHAPTER 4

Control

Please take a moment to get comfortable, relaxed, slow your breathing and let your body feel completely relaxed and your mind focused ready to absorb the final element of our formula, the element of Control.

As we said in our introduction, Control is the script that allows the formula to work, it is the framework around which Focus and Congruence can function, it is the glue that holds it all together. So let me start this section with a story and a question. Question first. Do you ever feel that events are controlling you? That you feel powerless in the face of a string of disasters or mishaps? That you want to shout "WHY ME?" I think there are times when it has happened to all of us, so I want to show you how often **you can** exert control if you want to.

To paraphrase the poet *"God give me the strength to change what I can and accept that which I cannot"* For **Acceptance** you may be surprised to learn, can also be a form of control; more of which later. Now, to the story which concerns a friend of mine, Stuart.

Stuart was always in a rush in the morning. The alarm would go off and not being a morning person he would press the snooze button to give himself another ten minutes of shut eye. Then when the alarm rang again he would get up, shower, shave, dress, have a quick coffee and cereal, dash out the house and drive to work; cursing the traffic jam all the way. He usually arrived at work just on time or a few minutes late, would rush to open his PC and then spend an hour processing his emails which made him late for the project he was looking after. This was very much the pattern of Stuart's life till one disastrous day.

Same scene, the alarm rang, he snoozed and got up, but as he did get up he stubbed his toe. The pain made his hand shake and rushing to shave he cut himself and then wasted more time covering it up. By the time he went downstairs, for his coffee, he was late, rushing, not concentrating and misjudged when he poured his coffee and spilt some on the work surface and floor. Cursing, he cleared it up and by the time he got to his car now fifteen minutes late he tried to start it but over revved it and it stalled. Finally, when he was on his way traffic was crawling, he was angry, frustrated and by the time he got to work late was in a foul mood. Rushing to turn on his PC he didn't wait for it to start up properly, pushed too many keys and the PC crashed. At this point he said "WHY ME?" and felt as if life had dealt him a crazy day. Of course, the rest of the day followed the same negative pattern.

So, let me ask you, does any of that sound familiar? Are you saying, we all get lousy days, what can you do? Well it has happened to all of us but bear with me. Let's re run the story; only this time, inserting CONTROL into it. You might be surprised at the outcome.

Let's start with the alarm going off and Stuart pressing the snooze button. He thinks he is getting an extra ten minutes of sleep. Actually, he is **wasting** ten minutes and not really sleeping. So, control change number one. By the way if this is you maybe try this. When the alarm goes off, lie there, take a deep breath, that way from the start you exert control and are not just reacting to the alarm, then get up. You now have bought yourself ten extra precious minutes instead of wasting them. Ok, back to the story. So Stuart gets up and stubs his toe. If he was in control he would have known that the pain caused a shot of adrenaline and Cortisol to course through his body which speeded up his system [by the way the reason for that is that any pain triggers and ancient fight or flight part of the brain which releases these two chemical into the system]. By exerting control, taking a second, realising the drugs in his system will make him shaky, he exerts control and calms himself before doing anything else. In this state of control and awareness he would not have cut himself shaving or spilt the coffee because of his Adrenalin induced shaky hands. Now he can leave home ten minutes early not fifteen minutes late. Traffic is lighter as it's earlier, and is therefore less frustrating. He arrives at work early and in control, opens his PC normally and has extra time to deal with his emails. Now Stuart feels ahead of the day and In Control and so his day naturally keeps getting better

Though this is a story, these are all real examples. We have far more control, as I hope you can see, over our circumstances than we realise. Take a moment to consider how the rules of control in this story might apply to your life. Is there somewhere you could use these examples of Control and indeed take more control of your life?

I said earlier that **Acceptance** can be a form of control. Let's take the traffic jam as an example. We have all experienced them, sat in them, got frustrated by them. Now despite leaving early or late, trying alternate routes, sometimes we will still be stuck in that jam. The uncontrolled reactive, non congruent reaction is to get frustrated, angry, nervous. Here is a situation you can do nothing about, so why fight it? The controlled response is to say "All right I'm in a jam, I can't do anything about it, so how can I use my time effectively?" With that attitude you are now in control and you can use the time to do breathing and relaxation exercises, listen to a CD, or the radio or review what you need to do that day. What you do is up to you, the point is, you have accepted the problem over which you have no control and turned it into an opportunity to do what you want.

It means the Jam far from being a frustrating, energy sapping experience is transformed into a useful positive space for you to relax and so when you finally arrive at your destination you will be in a positive congruent mood ready for the day; as opposed to an angry frustrated nervous state sapped of energy and happiness. Does that make sense, could you apply this to that and other situations? Do you see how control and acceptance can transform situations from negative draining ones to positive energising ones. Try it and see, I know you will feel the difference.

Just think about this example and apply it to anything in your day that is relevant. Could you take control there? Of course you can, try it next time you have a similar problem and you will feel the change. Like Congruence and Focus, the more you identify times to use it and practice I the easier it becomes.

Physical and Psychological Control

I hope you are getting the idea of how control will change your life and make it better. Let's just explore now a couple of different types of control. Physical control and Psychological control. Physical control is anything from working out in the gym for the full time you have allowed yourself to not spitting out a tasteless piece of food in front of a guest. Physical control is about you controlling your body not the other way around. Even down to being ill on some occasions. How often do we feel "1 degree under" yet convince ourselves we feel worse than we really do. Physical control allows us to realise how we really feel and function effectively within real constraints not bow to a sickness which is not as severe as we pretend.

That is of course linked to psychological control. If we control our mind then we will not succumb to the weak feeling of "Oh I'll stay in bed" when you know you should not, or not perform a task you know you should. Psychological control is about being honest and knowing that we can do more than we think we need to or are capable of doing.

The ultimate examples are: a mother lifting a heavy weight to free her child when normally she could never lift it or another example, going without sleep for long periods, say when nursing a sick child or being in the emergency services or the military. I am sure you can think of many other examples yourself can't you? The point is, we can either allow circumstances to dictate our actions and give in to self defeating assumptions such as "I can't .swim, write, pass that exam" and so on **OR take control and with focus and congruence honestly decide to take positive honest action.**

So, there we have it "CONTROL". The framework for the formula, the map that shows the direction we have to go, the frame within which we will succeed. Control is about taking positive active control of your life whatever the circumstance. Taking responsibility and removing blame. You are in control if you want to be, no one and nothing else can prevent or block that.

So, take a few minutes to think about Control and

how you can assert it for yourself in all areas of your life. Next we will draw all three elements of the formula together.

CHAPTER 5

The Coalesce

Introduction

The first step in our journey is nearly over. We have looked individually at the three elements of the ultimate formula for a happy life. Focus, Congruent and Control. I hope by now you begin to see and feel how applying this formula really will make your life happier and healthier. Of course in this handbook it is impossible to cover every example, possibility or problem, however by the end of this course, you will have all the tools you need to start on your new journey to health and ultimate happiness!!

We begin this final section where all elements will coalesce into a single unit that you will realise is far greater than the sum of its parts. We will begin this coalescence by reviewing each of the three elements. Then we will look at how together they combat every day problems such as stress, taking things personally, changes in one's life and external pressures and influence. After that we will see what the formula correctly applied gives in terms of clear goals, maximum energy and complete control. We will understand how this inevitably leads to health and happiness and finally look at the only tools you will ever need to apply this formula; honesty, a will to change and a desire to continually be better.

Focus

That's it, so let's review the three elements and first we looked at Focus. Focus is the searchlight that illuminates the path we choose to travel. We considered its five elements. To remind you these are: first **to identify a clear goal** and I reminded you that you need to be completely honest with yourself as to what that goal is. I suggested that if you found it difficult to identify; to spend time imagining a series of goals, two, five and ten years hence till you found the one that really fits like a glove. The second of the five elements of focus is **clarifying the clear path to achieve your goal.** Here as we explored together, you need to organise your thoughts and actions so that your focus is concentrated on the light that is your goal. Anything that contributes to reaching the light must be embraced; whatever seeks to divert you, or tries to block the light must be totally rejected. All your focus must be on the path to that goal. If you allow others or other ideas to divert you, you will fall off the path and find it difficult to get back on to it and continue in the direction you want. **Stick To The Path** wherever it takes you; if your goal is honest then focus on that and you will find all else will fall into place.

The third element of focus is, as we saw, **deciding on the resources you need to achieve your goal**. Be your own film director, make sure that to shoot your film and stay on your path, that all the resources you need, physical, emotional and psychological are in place in time to help you continue your journey and achieve your goal. Don't be distracted, focus on the resources you NEED not other things you might just fancy.

The fourth element of Focus is as we said sometimes the most difficult to achieve and that is as I am sure you remember, **taking the first step.** Don't let self defeating thoughts or negative people stop you. Don't let the past bind you. If your goal is honest, **then live in the now seize the day** and take that first step. That's all you have to do. Once you start, like a boulder rolling down hill it becomes easier ands easier and more and more joyous. **Don't hesitate:- The change you want is there waiting for you: Step into the light, go for your goal, you will succeed and be happier and healthier as a result.**

The final element of Focus is as you recall, **sticking to your journey.** Now that you are on the road, the closer to your goal you get the happier and healthier you will feel. Your goal is a magnet drawing you forward. Stick with the energy the right path gives you. Do not be diverted. Once on your path focus on it and everything that moves you forward and reject anything and anyone that tries to divert you from your goal or blocks your path. Stay with the journey, Focus on the goal and your physical, emotional and psychological happiness will continue to increase.

So there we have Focus, now making sure you are still relaxed, breathing slowly and deeply and your mind is sharp and focused let us review being Congruent.

Congruent

Being Congruent is being in harmony; harmony of mind, body and soul; physical, emotional and psychological harmony. When you are congruent all your energy flows together and in the same direction without let or hindrance. *It feels like your whole body, mind and soul are superheated, energised;* you have more energy, are healthier and so much happier, you will find you cannot stop smiling!

All of us have had at least one experience like that,

maybe as a child or as an adult, alone or with someone. Think of that time when you were like that: happy, smiling, energised full of positive love and energy-you can have that feeling more and more, the more congruent you become. Isn't that a wonderful thought? Avoid anything or anyone you can that drains you or exudes negative vibes; if its work that drags you down; are you in the right job? If it's a person, are you in the right relationship? If it's a place, are you in the right location for you?

If you need to use willpower, do you remember, you are **not** Congruent because you are fighting against yourself. As we saw, this is a battle you cannot ever truly win. You might achieve short term success but you will slip into long term failure or disappointment. It's like a person who said, "Of course I Can give up smoking, it's easy, I've done it ten times."

We also explored together physical congruence and looked at diet, exercise sleep, relaxation and freedom from stress. We reviewed the triggers to stress, how to identify them and how to relax, to help you maximise your physical congruence.

Being congruent in the body was one element and we also looked at being congruent in mind and soul. For that congruence there must be a harmony between what you think and what you feel. We looked at impulse shopping and the battle between common sense, the mind and desire, the emotion. We used an exercise to help you be congruent, I am sure you recall it.

Every time you feel a conflict between emotion and the psychological, between mind and soul, **STOP, Take a deep breath and take a second to examine what is really causing the conflict. In that second YOU WILL KNOW WHAT IS RIGHT; and that is your action, your true path**. Real

congruence makes you feel good forever, incongruent impulses only give short term satisfaction and long term resentment and guilt. The more you do this simple exercise, listen to your conscience, and are guided by it, the more congruent you will become and the happier and healthier you will feel.

Control

So now let's review the final element in the ultimate formula for a happy life – **Control**

Control is the frame that allows the formula FCO^2 to coalesce and to work. It is the glue that holds focus and being congruent together. In Stuart's story we saw how we actually have more control over our lives than we sometimes realise – do you remember, I am sure you do. We also saw that **Acceptance** is also a form of control as in the example of the traffic jam. Accept you cannot change all events and use your time positively instead of succumbing to stress and frustration. We looked at physical control of our bodies and not giving in to physical or psychological weakening thoughts and feelings. Applying honest control to our actions to allow us to do what we have to do.

Control is about being positive and proactive. Control is about taking responsibility for yourself and not blaming others or outside forces. Control is about seeing the positive and acting in a positive manner even in situations you cannot change. **Take control of your life and with Focus and being Congruent you are invincible. For whatever happens, no one will be able to affect or disrupt the essential focused, congruent you!**

So by focusing on a clear goal and focusing on the

path needed to achieve it, by being honest and congruent so all your energy flows together in one powerful uninterrupted stream; and by exercising control over yourself and your surroundings, you will begin to live a life filled by positives, moving in a direction you want; mind, body and soul working together in such a powerful way that you will achieve all that you want. On that wondrous journey, free from stress and negativity your physical, psychological and emotional well being will improve incredibly. Yes, just being on the journey will increase your happiness and make you feel more alive and more healthy.

Apply this formula honestly, sincerely and completely and you will know true happiness and realise FCO^2 is indeed the ultimate formula for a happy life.

How are you feeling? I hope as energised and excited and optimistic as I am. Writing this handbook filled me with increased energy and hope and I hope you feel the same. If you are convinced then that is it. Go away, practice what you have learnt, use the handbook to remind you and help energise you anew, and use the exercises to hep you relax, sleep better and keep free from stress. Enjoy a wonderful life full of glorious sunrises.

CHAPTER 6

Afterthought

For those of you that would like some more information, then stay with me as we explore a few points. Consider this an after thought to the coalesce.

COMBATTING STRESS

First: FCO^2 can help combat stress; if you apply the rules of being congruent and the relaxation exercises as well as the trigger identification exercise you will considerably reduce pressure turning into stress, with all the physical downside, such as headaches. muscle aches and being generally run down.

NOT TAKING THINGS PERSONALLY

Second: Applying FCO^2 allows you, by staying focused, being congruent and maintaining control to take things less personally. When people put you down, insult or diminish you; realise it is just a reflection of their weakness. If you apply the formula, stay focused, congruent and in control you realise the comments and actions of those people are their problem, not a reflection of you and therefore cannot touch you. FCO^2 is your armour against negativity, insults or bullying, apply it fully and no one will or can harm you, you will remain strong in yourself whatever the outside world hurls at you.

EMBRACING CHANGE

Third: Some of us fear change, yet just by reading this handbook and applying the formula you KNOW that change, if it is towards a goal you truly desire is good and positive and to be embraced. Change happens every second of every minute of every hour of every day. Apply the formula, embrace it, use it, revel in it, NEVER FEAR IT!

RESISTING OUTSIDE INFLUENCE

And Fourth: Applying FCO² means you will no longer be prey to outside pressure and influence. Secure, congruent, focused and in control **YOU** make the decisions, you control the rudder of your ship and no outside current or force can drag you off course or have power over you.

What does FCO² give you as well? It gives you the tools to define and achieve your true goals.

EXTRA ENERGY

It gives you more energy than you have ever had before. Energy in your mind, your body and your soul. You will find you wake up with a smile, looking forward to the day and with boundless energy, able to achieve all you need as a focused, congruent and in control being, excited by the challenges of reaching your goals and continuing your journey.

The formula gives you the tools to acquire and maintain control of yourself and your situation. All of this leads to greater health as all your energies flow together; your body is physically relaxed, your mind uncluttered and unstressed. You will even age slower. Stress ages the body fast, being congruent and relaxed helps your health, wellbeing and youth. If that was not enough, FCO² will make you happy. Apply it – you will feel it working and know it is indeed the ultimate formula for a happy life and I am honoured to share it with you and impart something that will make your life so much better and happier. You may find smiling so much begins to hurt, though I don't think that's much of a sacrifice, do you?

THE TOOLS YOU NEED

Finally, what tools do you need to apply this formula? They are simple and essential, the good news is, you possess them already. They are:

HONESTY	Be totally honest with yourself, you will find it invigorating
THE WILL	If you have read this far you DO want to change – so now
TO CHANGE	You can and will.
DESIRE TO	The honest desire to always strive to be better.
ALWAYS BE	As long as you don't want to be stuck in a rut, then
BETTER	You have this desire, use it, enjoy it.

There you have it, FCO^2 the ultimate formula for a happy life. I know when you apply the formula, your life will improve and you will as you apply it, become happier and healthier. It has been a privilege helping you find the way. I wish you all, every success and joy as you follow your path to you goal in a focused, congruent direction, in control of yourself now and in the future.

Let the journey begin-good luck and I leave you with a final thought, a poem:

> *"Life is a journey we all have to take*
> *Life is the Now the reality we make*
> *Life is choices we all have to take*
> *Life is the joy only honesty creates*
>
> *Focus is the light that illuminates our way*
> *Congruence the harmony that will always stay*
> *Control the framework for each single day*
> *And Now the only time to act as we may"*
> Bruce

I'm Bruce Lawson and you have been reading FCO^2 the ultimate formula for a happy life.

Appendices

Please note you can just read these exercises or record
them onto your MP3 player and listen to them.

www.a-lifetime-of-sunrises.co.uk

Relaxation Exercise

Let us take a minute to together enjoy a moment of rest and relaxation.

As you listen to my voice sit comfortably and relaxed close your eyes and allow yourself a few minutes of Total warm and complete relaxation: let's just get our breathing relaxed too with this exercise you know so well now:

Breathe in – hold for 2 seconds think count of 1 – breathe out slowly and deeply

Breathe in – hold for 2 seconds think count of 2 – breathe out slowly and deeply

Breathe in – hold for 2 seconds think count of 3 – breathe out slowly and deeply – and as you breathe out think about how your body is relaxing

Breathe in – hold for 2 seconds think count of 4 – breathe out slowly and deeply – and feel how heavy your feet feel against the ground

Breathe in – hold for 2 seconds think count of

5 – breathe out slowly and deeply – and feel how heavy your thighs feel against the chair and how relaxed

Breathe in – hold for 2 seconds think count of 6 – breathe out slowly and deeply – if your eyes feel heavy and you want to close them at any time **DO SO NOW** or whenever

Breathe in – hold for 2 seconds think count of 7 – breathe out slowly and deeply – and feel how heavy and relaxed your back and bottom feel against the chair heavy and relaxed like your closed eyes

Breathe in – hold for 2 seconds think count of 8 – breathe out slowly and deeply – and feel how heavy your arms and shoulders feel heavy and totally relaxed with each breath

Breathe in – hold for 2 seconds think count of 9 – breathe out slowly and deeply – and feel how your whole body feels relaxed from your feet to your head relaxed yet focused

Breathe in – hold for 2 seconds think count of 10 – breathe out slowly and deeply – and feel how your mind is clear and ready to learn while your body stays totally relaxed

Now just keep breathing slowly and deeply while your mind stays deeply focused on and your body continues to remain delightfully wonderfully relaxed.

Goal Clarification, Reinforcement and Motivation

As always it begins with breathing. As before sit in your chair.

Breathe in – hold for 2 seconds think count of 1 – breathe out slowly and deeply

Breathe in – hold for 2 seconds think count of 2 – breathe out slowly and deeply

Breathe in – hold for 2 seconds think count of 3 – breathe out slowly and deeply – and as you breathe out think about how your body is relaxing

Breathe in – hold for 2 seconds think count of 4 – breathe out slowly and deeply – and feel how heavy your feet feel against the ground

Breathe in – hold for 2 seconds think count of 5 – breathe out slowly and deeply – and feel

how heavy your thighs feel against the chair and how relaxed

Breathe in – hold for 2 seconds think count of 6 – breathe out slowly and deeply – if your eyes feel heavy and you want to close them at any time **DO SO NOW** or whenever

Breathe in – hold for 2 seconds think count of 7 – breathe out slowly and deeply – and feel how heavy and relaxed your back and bottom feel against the chair heavy and relaxed like your closed eyes

Breathe in – hold for 2 seconds think count of 8 – breathe out slowly and deeply – and feel how heavy your arms and shoulders feel heavy and totally relaxed with each breath

Breathe in – hold for 2 seconds think count of 9 – breathe out slowly and deeply – and feel how your whole body feels relaxed from your feet to your head relaxed yet focused

Breathe in – hold for 2 seconds think count of 10 – breathe out slowly and deeply – and feel how your mind is clear and ready to learn while your body stays totally relaxed

Now just keep breathing slowly and deeply while your mind stays deeply focused and your body continues to remain delightfully wonderfully relaxed.

Wonderful; now you are in the right frame to focus on the exercise of imagining you have achieved your goal. You can repeat this exercise whenever you want to reinforce your motivation to your goal.

I want you to imagine your goal and how you will be when you have achieved it – whatever you have decided it is. SEE IT, EXPLORE ITS COLOURS, FEEL ITS EMOTIONS, ITS PHYSICALITY; LISTEN TO THE SOUNDS THAT SURROUND IT. And as your goal becomes more vibrant and clear, enjoy the wonderful depth of positive happiness. The deep emotion of well being achieving this goal gives. Take some time to explore your goal and the pleasure achieving it brings, the completeness, the peace, the satisfaction the inner calm. It is a warm woolly sweater that embraces and protects you, a harmonious sound that surrounds and relaxes you, a feeling of completeness and peace and warmth that keeps you safe and secure. Enjoy this knowing you can return to it at any time.

AND NOW BEGIN TO WORK BACK MOVING IN TIME AND IMAGINE WHAT STEPS YOU NEED TO REACH THAT WONDERFUL GOAL. As you take each step back, look at each action necessary to keep you on that clear path to that goal. At each step, feel the emotional satisfaction of the right step and the right action on that path, the right decision made and stuck to. See each right decision, each correct step, its vibrant colour, listen to the positive sound of the right action stated aloud, and feel throughout your body how good and right each correct decision was following the right path reinforcing the road to your goal.

Carry on journeying back seeing each step, feeling each decision, sounding out every thought until you arrive at **TODAY**.

Now take a deep breath and in an instant review your journey. If that instant review makes you smile, makes your body feel good then you have your clear path. If anything strikes a sour note then stop. And when ready repeat the exercise till everything is congruent and you **KNOW** in every fibre of your body, mind and soul that your path is right, your aim is true.

Now you can open your eyes – enjoy the wonderful sensation of right focused decision.

Repeat this exercise any time you need to top up your motivation or give yourself a dose of warm wonder.

Sleep Exercise

Ok – so for this exercise you need to be lying on your bed, ready for sleep. Lie on your back, lights dim or off and with no distractions if possible like the radio or TV; noisy neighbours, screaming kids-you get the idea. Are you ready, lying on your back, comfortable, excellent then lets begin.

This is an exercise in relaxation of body and mind and by the end you will be able to fall naturally into a deep relaxed sleep. As you are lying there first begin by getting your breathing slow and steady. You know how. Breathe in slowly and deeply hold for two seconds and breathe out fully. Lets first repeat that ten times to get you full relaxed

Then after that we will use tensing and relaxing our body to ensure you fall easily and naturally into a wonderful deep satisfying sleep. At any time when you feel yourself slipping into sleep let it happen you do not need to complete the exercise just let the voice run on in the background as you fall deeply asleep.

Breathe in – hold for 2 seconds think count of 1 – breathe out slowly and deeply

Breathe in – hold for 2 seconds think count of 2 – breathe out slowly and deeply

Breathe in – hold for 2 seconds think count of 3 – breathe out slowly and deeply – and as you breathe out think about how your body is relaxing

Breathe in – hold for 2 seconds think count of 4 – breathe out slowly and deeply – and feel how heavy your feet feel resting on the bed

Breathe in – hold for 2 seconds think count of 5 – breathe out slowly and deeply – and feel how heavy your thighs feel against the bed and how relaxed

Breathe in – hold for 2 seconds think count of 6 – breathe out slowly and deeply – if your eyes feel heavy and you want to close them at any time DO SO NOW or whenever

Breathe in – hold for 2 seconds think count of 7 – breathe out slowly and deeply – and feel how heavy and relaxed your back and bottom feel against the bed heavy and relaxed like your closed eyes

Breathe in – hold for 2 seconds think count of 8 – breathe out slowly and deeply – and feel how heavy your arms and shoulders feel heavy

and totally relaxed with each breath

Breathe in – hold for 2 seconds think count of 9 – breathe out slowly and deeply – and feel how your whole body feels relaxed from your feet to your head relaxed at peace

Breathe in – hold for 2 seconds think count of 10 – breathe out slowly and deeply – and feel how your mind is quiet and ready for sleep while your body stays deeply totally relaxed

Now just keep breathing slowly and deeply while your mind stays deeply quiet and your body continues to remain delightfully wonderfully deeply relaxed.

Wonderful – keeping your breathing relaxed and slow feel yourself drifting off into sleep.

Start with your toes and tense and relax your left toes twice, that's it tense and relax, tense and relax.

Now your left foot, tense and relax, tense and relax.

Now move up to your left leg, tense and relax, tense and relax,

Now your left thigh, tense and relax, tense and relax; that's it feel how wonderfully heavy and relaxed your body is and how peaceful and quiet your mind is, still focusing just on my voice on tensing and relaxing, nothing else.

Now your chest, tense and relax tense and relax, that's it..

Now your left shoulder tense and relax, tense and relax,

Now your left arm, tense and relax, tense and relax, yes and now your left hand, tense and relax, tense and relax, excellent slowly drifting to sleep your body wonderfully heavy, your eyes heavy and relaxed, your mind at peace as you clench and relax your eyelids tense and relax as your eyes stay firmly deeply shut...

And now the right side of your body as before starting with your right toes:

Start with your toes and tense and relax your right toes twice, that's it tense and relax, tense and relax.

Now your right foot, tense and relax, tense and relax.

Now move up to your right leg, tense and relax, tense and relax,

Now your right thigh, tense and relax, tense and relax; that's it feel how wonderfully heavy and relaxed your body is and how peaceful and quiet your mind is still focusing just on my voice on tensing and relaxing nothing else..

Now your chest tense and relax tense and relax, that's it..

Now your right shoulder tense and relax, tense and relax,

Now your right arm, tense and relax, tense and relax yes and

Now your right hand, tense and relax, tense and relax, excellent slowly drifting to sleep your body wonderfully heavy, your eyes heavy and relaxed, your mind at peace as you clench and relax your eyelids tense and relax as your eyes stay firmly deeply shut... as you fall into a deep relaxed warm and wonderful natural sleep, sleeping through the night your body and mind rested and at peace so that you will wake refreshed and energised ready for a wonderful new day

Stress Relief Exercise

As you listen to my voice sit or stand or lie comfortably and relaxed close your eyes if its safe to do so and allow yourself a few minutes of Total warm and complete relaxation free from any stress that might be near:-let's just get our breathing relaxed too with this exercise you know so well now:

Breathe in – hold for 2 seconds think count of 1 – breathe out slowly and deeply

Breathe in – hold for 2 seconds think count of 2 – breathe out slowly and deeply

Breathe in – hold for 2 seconds think count of 3 – breathe out slowly and deeply – and as you breathe out think about how your body is relaxing

Breathe in – hold for 2 seconds think count of 4 – breathe out slowly and deeply – and feel how heavy your feet feel against the ground – and now See your body as a strong oak tree. Your body is solid like the wide, brown trunk

of the tree. Imagine sturdy roots growing from your legs and going down deeply into the earth, anchoring your body. You feel solid and strong, able to handle any stress.

Breathe in – hold for 2 seconds think count of 5 – breathe out slowly and deeply – and feel how heavy your thighs feel and how relaxed and strong anchored to the earth like a strong wide powerful oak tree you feel

Breathe in – hold for 2 seconds think count of 6 – breathe out slowly and deeply – if your eyes feel heavy and you want to close them at any time **DO SO NOW** or whenever letting your energy flow through you grounding you to the earth as an oak tree and its roots stay grounded to the earth

Breathe in – hold for 2 seconds think count of 7 – breathe out slowly and deeply – and feel how heavy and relaxed the rest of your body feels with energy flowing from top to bottom, relaxed and calm grounded in the earth as the oak tree strong and powerful.

Breathe in – hold for 2 seconds think count of 8 – breathe out slowly and deeply – and feel how heavy your arms and shoulders feel heavy and totally relaxed with each breath, energy flowing calmly through from your head to your toes, your feet in contact with the ground grounded in the earth as the oak tree has its roots grounded in the soil.

Breathe in – hold for 2 seconds think count of 9 – breathe out slowly and deeply – and feel how your whole body feel relaxed from your feet to your head relaxed yet focused

Breathe in – hold for 2 seconds think count of 10 – breathe out slowly and deeply – and feel how your mind is clear and calm free from tension or stress, your body and mind ready to continue whatever the situation, grounded an calm, strong as the oak, grounded and aware and safe and secure as the oak tree, able to stay calm and relaxed whatever the situation.

Now just keep breathing slowly and deeply while your mind stays deeply calm your body continues to remain delightfully wonderfully relaxed.

Wonderful – now you are in the right frame to continue: Now you can open your eyes – enjoy the wonderful sensation of strength, and calm, totally relaxed and able to deal with whatever situation presents itself.

Tips for a Stress-free Lifestyle

Breathing

Though breathing comes naturally, deep breathing is often overlooked as an exercise, it's an excellent stress reducer. Breathe in while tucking in your tummy and feel the air as it expands your lungs and your chest. Breathe in to the count of three and hold it for two counts. Then exhale to the count of three. Take two to three deep breathes several times a day and soon daily stress triggers may well be blown away.

Take a brief walk in your lunch or coffee break

A brisk ten or fifteen minute walk each day is not only physically good for you but moves your focus from your problems to the scenery around you and aids as a distraction and stimulant.

Stand and stretch

Visualize the stress flooding from your back, legs, your shoulders, and pour out of your fingertips and toes. .

Movement

Join an aerobics class, a martial arts one or just dance at

home. Dancing has a two advantages, exercise, and it is a great stress reducer.

Stress at Work – tips on how to control it

Stress at work is common and damaging too many of us. Stress results in a decrease in job satisfaction, motivation, reduced production, and increased conflicts, which inevitably lead to more stress! If you ignore stress signals, you are more liable to become ill or fatigued and to experience injury. As an employee, there are several steps you can take to preserve your health by reducing workplace stress.

External triggers

Stress can be caused by something that seems as small as an incorrectly positioned chair or computer screen. Other examples of external triggers include loud or continuous noise, overheated or cold conditions, nosy or noisy co-workers, demanding bosses, and complaining customers. If external triggers are causing problems for you, the worst thing you can do is ignore them. Identifying and examine external triggers for possible solutions. Even if all of them aren't resolved, any positive change you will result in a happier, healthier you.

Internal triggers

Internal triggers can be feelings of irritability, dissatisfaction, inability, or the feeling that your efforts aren't properly rewarded or recognized. One helpful way to reduce internal stress is to remember what you liked about your job when you started it. Consider what has changed as well as what needs to change for you to be satisfied again.

Other tips to avoid stress at work
Condition yourself to wake and get ready, not for work, but for your day.

Driving to work, listen to music, comedy, self help CDs – anything that isn't related to work.

Take an alternative route to your work. A change in scenery will help you stay alert and keep you focused. .

Instead of coffee, drink water, juice, or electrolyte infused drinks. Dehydration often is the cause of fatigue. Coffee and soft drinks that contain caffeine may seem to "keep you going", but in reality they add to stress and don't keep your body hydrated.

As you plan your work, plan your time away from work. At the end of the day, leave work behind you and focus on your plans for the evening. Work to live. Relaxation away from work means less stress… and a better day tomorrow!

More tips to avoid stress – a relaxation exercise

Planning your relaxation reduces anxiety and helps your body and mind recover from everyday stress. A long soak in a bath, music or a walk in the park do the trick for some but for others try a relaxation or meditation class.

22 Stress Reducing tips that work

1.   Get up fifteen minutes earlier in the morning. The inevitable morning mishaps will be less stressful.

2.   Prepare for the morning the evening before. Set the breakfast table, make lunches, select and leave out the clothes you plan to wear.

3.   Write down appointment times, don't rely on your memory when to collect items or do chores.

4.   Be prepared to wait. A paperback can make a wait in a post office line almost pleasant.

5.   Procrastination is stressful. Whatever you want to do tomorrow, do today; whatever you want to do today, do it now.

6.   Allow extra time to get to appointments.

7.   Eliminate (or restrict) the amount of caffeine in your diet.

8.   Always set up contingency plans, "just in case".

9.   Relax your standards. The world will not end if the house doesn't get completely cleaned this weekend.

10.   Say "No!" Saying "no" to extra activities or events you don't have time for reduces stress; everyone needs quiet time to relax and be alone.

11.   Unplug your phone. Want to take a long bath, meditate, sleep, or read without interruption? Drum up the courage to temporarily disconnect. (The possibility of

there being a terrible emergency in the next hour or so is almost nil.) Or use an answering machine.

12. Get enough sleep

13. Talk about it. Discussing your problems can help clear your mind of confusion so you can concentrate on problem solving.

14. Learn to live one day at a time. Live in the Now

15. Every day, do one thing you really enjoy.

16. Do something for somebody else.

17. Become more flexible.

18. Eliminate destructive self-talk: or self limiting statements

19. Do one thing at a time. When you are with someone, be with that person and with no one or nothing else. When you are busy with a project, concentrate on doing that project and forget about everything else you have to do..

20. If an especially unpleasant task faces you, do it early in the day and get it over with, then the rest of your day will be free of anxiety.

21. Learn to delegate responsibility to capable others. Have a forgiving view of events and people. Accept the fact that we live in an imperfect world.

22. Have an optimistic view of the world. Believe that most people are doing the best they can.

Tips for an Easy Sleep Routine

If you are having problems falling asleep, or wake up too many times in the night, or your sleep is interrupted or not try the following tips:

- **Listen to Relaxation CDs**. Some people find natural sounds, such as the ocean or forest, to be soothing for sleep.
- **EFT** Most people can learn this gentle tapping technique in several minutes. Emotional freedom technique can reduce stress, and aid restful sleep
- **Avoid before-bed snacks,**. These will raise blood sugar and inhibit sleep.
- **Sleep in as complete darkness as possible**. If there is even the tiniest bit of light in the room it can disrupt your circadian rhythm and your pineal gland's production of melatonin and seratonin.
- **No TV right before bed**. It is too stimulating to the brain and it will take longer to fall asleep.
- **Read something spiritual or**

religious. This will help you to relax..

- **Get to bed as early as possible**. Our systems, particularly the adrenals, do a majority of their recharging or recovering during the hours of 11PM and 1AM. people would go to bed shortly after sundown, which nature intended for humans .

- **Take a hot bath, shower or sauna before bed**

- **Don't drink any fluids within 2 hours of going to bed**.

- **Reduce or avoid as many drugs as possible**.

- **Avoid caffeine**..

- **Avoid alcohol**.

- **Check your bedroom for electro-magnetic fields (EMFs)**.

- **Keep the temperature in the bedroom no higher than 18 degrees C**.

- **Make certain you are exercising regularly**.

- **Expose yourself to sunlight during the day. Sunlight is a power cue that sets your circadian clock. Having a strong circadian rhythm helps you sleep more soundly at night.**

Visualisation Exercise: Finding a safe place

We use visualization everyday. You may, for example, daydream about a beautiful place you want to go for a holiday. These images usually put us in a positive mood and create feelings of relaxation. Visualization exercises can have the same effect. The technique is simple to learn and works quickly. Use it to reduce anxiety or whenever you are in a stressful situation. For this exercise, feel free to be as imaginative as you want in creating the scenery in your mind. It's normal that your mind will wander. Just allow yourself to passively come back to your imagery Read, remember and practice these steps. When you're ready, spend the next 15 to 20 minutes to create the scenery of your choice in your mind.

A] Sit or lie down in a comfortable position.

B] Close your eyes.

C] Begin to breathe slowly and evenly allowing your breathing to slow and your body to relax.

D] Now create an image in your mind of some place where you felt truly relaxed, calm, safe and happy. It could be a beach, a wood, by a stream. A mountain top or a desert island, whatever your imagination gives you.

E]   In this image, observe what is happening. Notice the colours of the scenery. Notice the quiet atmosphere, or movement of the air. Notice the shapes of familiar objects, and be aware of any movement that is taking place. Listen to any sounds there might be and any feelings under your feet, or through your hands like wind blowing or sand through your toes.

F]   Go on imagining this scene. Continue to breathe deeply and evenly. Allow yourself to recall the most minute details of the experience. Remember the sights, the sounds, the smells, the feelings, and the mood. Just let yourself re-experience the moments. Breathe deeply and evenly. Just relax and enjoy the memory. Create as vivid and real a place as you can, a place of safety and calm, of happiness, a special place.

G]   Recall the positive feelings in that scene. Enjoy what you remember and what you see in your mind's eye. Breathe deeply and relax. When you are ready and relaxed open your eyes and continue to feel the calm safe feelings you had knowing you can return to your safe place any time you want to.

H]   The purpose of the safe place is to be able to go there automatically when things start to get a bit rough. It takes a lot of practice – you have to return there as many times as you can.

I]   Each time you return to your safe place explore it in more detail. Experience more of the sights and sounds, the smells and touch, the scenery and wildlife.

J]   Each time you visit it will become richer and be easier to get there. After practice you will be able to go there without effort and enjoy its calm and safety for as long as you need.

ABOUT THE AUTHOR

Bruce Lawson has over 30 years in training, coaching, counselling, sales and personal development. He is a Master practitioner of NLP a certified Hypnotherapist with GHC, a qualified practitioner of EFT and is creator of the FCO^2® and COPE® systems of personal happiness and individual development. Bruce has worked in the UK and abroad and has a deep interest in our diverse spiritual roots and their link to current psychology.

This is his first book which offers everyone the chance to real personal fulfilment and happiness by applying a simple formula developed out of Bruce's extensive experience and research.

For more information email Bruce at:
alifetimeofsunrises@hotmail.co.uk

or visit his website
www.a-lifetime-of-sunrises.co.uk